RIDE THE WIND

AIRBORNE JOURNEYS OF ANIMALS AND PLANTS

by Seymour Simon   *Illustrated by* Elsa Warnick

Browndeer Press
Harcourt Brace & Company
San Diego   New York   London

Requests for permission to make copies of any part of the work should be
mailed to: Permissions Department, Harcourt Brace & Company,
6277 Sea Harbor Drive, Orlando, Florida 32887-6777.

Browndeer Press is a registered trademark of Harcourt Brace & Company.

Library of Congress Cataloging-in-Publication Data
Simon, Seymour.
Ride the wind: airborne journeys of animals and plants;
illustrated by Elsa Warnick.—1st ed.
p.   cm.
"Browndeer Press."
ISBN 0-15-292887-1
1. Animal migration—Juvenile literature. 2. Plants—Migration—Juvenile literature.
3. Animal flight—Juvenile literature. 4. Seeds—Dispersal—Juvenile literature.
[1. Animals—Migration. 2. Animal flight. 3. Seeds—Dispersal.]
I. Warnick, Elsa, ill.   II. Title.
QL754.S56   1997
591.52'5—dc20   94-29052

First edition
F E D C B A

Printed in Singapore

The illustrations in this book were done in watercolor on
Fabriano Artistico, 140-lb. cold press, 100% cotton paper.
The text type was set in Meridien.
Title calligraphy by John Stevens
Color separations by Bright Arts, Ltd., Singapore
Printed and bound by Tien Wah Press, Singapore
This book was printed on Nymolla Matte Art paper.
Production supervision by Stanley Redfern and Pascha Gerlinger
Designed by Judythe Sieck

For Joyce and Florence
and their adorable granddaughter Chloe
—S. S.

For my beloved sons,
Matt and Milan Erceg
—E. W.

At any moment all over the world, animals and plants are sailing through the sky. Birds and butterflies soar, flap, glide, and flit on journeys of hundreds or thousands of miles. Locusts swarm by the millions, an airborne river of buzzing insects eating everything in their path. Bats flutter their skin-covered wings, zigzagging through the night sky. Some spiders are balloonists, floating on silken threads carried to great heights by the wind. Feathery dandelion tufts sail aloft on the gentlest breezes. Winged fruits and seeds whirl downward through the air, spinning like tiny helicopters.

All the animals and plants in the world live on the earth as well as above its surface. For our planet is made up not only of rocks, soil, and water, but also of the gases in its atmosphere. Animals and plants, and people, too, live at the bottom of the atmosphere—an enormous ocean of air that reaches hundreds of miles above the solid surface of Earth. Animals and plants that make air journeys travel through a layer of the atmosphere called the troposphere, which can be up to six miles high.

Air is a real substance, even though it is invisible. A bird's wing pushes against the air in its path and the air pushes back against the wing. Birds flap their wings to push through the air the way swimmers use their arms to push through water. The support of the air allows birds, bats, and insects to fly, and carries seeds and ballooning spiders aloft.

Birds and bats are the only vertebrates—animals with backbones—that can truly fly. (Some animals, such as flying fish, can glide for short distances.) Because a bat's wing is a thin, skinlike substance supported by the long bones of the bat's fingers and arms, bats can vary the outline of their wings quickly and easily and thus make sudden turns in the air.

Bird feathers weigh very little and have a broad surface that catches the wind. Bird bones are often hollow and lightweight, and form a strong support for the flight feathers of a bird's wings. The breastbone of most birds supports the muscles used in flying; the muscles are the heaviest part of a bird's body.

Bird wings vary in shape. Some, like the gull's, are good for soaring as well as for strong and quick flight. Others, like the wings of the albatross, are broader for gliding, while still others, like those of the swift, are narrower for speed.

The seasonal journeys of large groups of animals are called migrations. Animals migrate when the weather becomes too cold or too hot, or when food is unavailable.

Among migrating birds, the Arctic tern is the long-distance champion of air travelers. Each year, adult terns fly from the Arctic to the Antarctic and back again. The round-trip journey of about twenty-five thousand miles takes eight months of almost nonstop flying. On its trip, the tern passes from a northern summer to a southern summer. When a tern arrives at its Arctic breeding grounds in spring, it returns to the same area it left the previous autumn.

In the autumn, terns from Greenland and Canada ride on westerly winds across the stormy Atlantic Ocean to Europe and then head south along the coast of West Africa. While traveling, terns plunge into the cold waters along their path to capture fish.

About February, adult terns begin their journey back to the Arctic. Most of the young birds remain in the south during their first year. By the third spring they fly back to the Arctic to find a mate and breed. As adults they will spend the rest of their lives—twenty to thirty years—following an endless summer around the world.

Some birds spend most of their lives on the wing. Along the edges of Antarctica, a big white bird glides effortlessly over great distances, searching the icy ocean waters for food. The wandering albatross may have a wingspan of eleven feet, the largest of any modern bird. Spotting a fish or squid, the bird drops to the water to feed and then is off into the air again. The albatross may journey over the southern oceans for distances up to twenty thousand miles during a ten-month span, following the prevailing westerly winds around Antarctica, and never once resting on dry land.

When breeding season comes in the spring (late September in the Southern Hemisphere, where the seasons are the reverse of those in the Northern Hemisphere), the albatross returns to the storm-tossed slopes and cliffs of Bird Island in the South Atlantic. The male lands first and may find the nest he and his mate have used for years—a small pile of mud and plant parts rimmed around the top to prevent an egg from rolling away. The female lands about a week later and the birds begin to court each other after their long separation. The male stays around the nest and feeds in the area, but the female takes to the air again and spends several months at sea eating as much food as she can. She will return in December or January and lay a single egg in the nest.

*H*alfway around the world to the north, the lesser snow goose, a beautiful large white bird with black wing tips, comes gliding to the Arctic tundra on the cold winds of late winter. Settling in huge colonies of thousands of pairs, the birds mate and the females lay their eggs. The chicks hatch in a few weeks and soon leave their nests to feed on newly sprouted marsh plants and grasses.

Summer does not last long in the Arctic. As the days shorten, flocks of honking, whistling, quacking snow geese take off in bursts of white feathers. The birds fly south in formations and touch down in central California in October. There they feed on water plants until the late winter, when they once again take to the air and return to their home in the north. Blue geese travel even longer distances than their cousins. Many blue geese spend the summer in breeding grounds in the far north Arctic. In autumn the blue geese journey southward to the coastal marshes in Texas and Louisiana. When they return in the spring, they take a path through the middle of North America, making a loop thousands of miles long.

The American golden plover makes an even longer loop migration, an incredible journey of more than twelve thousand miles. This small wading bird spends the summer at its breeding grounds on the tundra of far northern Canada. In late summer and early autumn, the plover heads southeast to the coast of Labrador and then journeys outward over the Atlantic Ocean to the northern coast of South America. Continuing its long flight, the plover wings its way south to spend the summer on the flat grasslands of Argentina. In the autumn, on its return journey to the north, the plover takes an entirely different route, mostly over land rather than water.

The young plovers that are born in the summer in the north don't follow the same route as the adults. Instead of flying the long and dangerous route across the Atlantic Ocean, the youngsters journey southward, taking an inland route that is just about the reverse of the northward path of the adults. This means that the path the plover follows changes with the age of the bird. Each young bird must be born with the ability not only to follow one route on its first migration south, but also to change to quite a different route for the rest of its life.

*J*ust like birds, many butterflies fly toward the Tropics in late summer and early autumn, and toward the Poles in the spring. Butterflies fluttering over grassy fields on a sunny day in the late summer are a common sight. It can be difficult to tell whether the butterflies are migrating or whether they live in the area. But every so often a butterfly may appear on one side of the field, fly straight across, and disappear on the other side. If it's small and white, it may be a cabbage white (a very common butterfly).

The life span of most butterflies that live in temperate climates is often less than three or four weeks. Small butterflies travel very slowly compared to some birds. In its entire lifetime a small cabbage white may travel only about one hundred miles. Along the way, the butterflies eat and mate and the females lay eggs.

The champion butterfly traveler is the monarch of North America. Hatched from a tiny egg on the underside of a milkweed leaf in southern Canada or the northern United States, the monarch emerges as a caterpillar in early summer. The tiger-striped caterpillar does little but eat milkweed leaves and grow larger. After shedding its skin several times, the caterpillar spins a silken chamber and becomes a pupa, or chrysalis. Finally the fully formed orange-brown, three- to four-inch monarch butterfly emerges.

A MONARCH'S LIFE

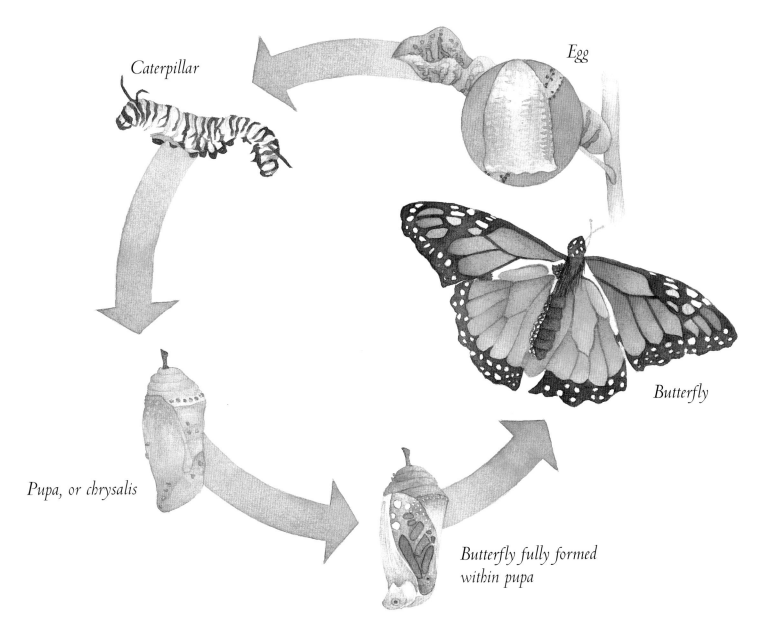

Caterpillar

Egg

Butterfly

Pupa, or chrysalis

Butterfly fully formed within pupa

*I*n July or early August, the monarchs take wing and begin a journey of hundreds of miles southward, to warmer places in Southern California. Some travel even farther—more than a thousand miles—to wintering sites along the Gulf of Mexico. The direction and time of year of the monarch's flight are so regular and predictable that many towns along the way celebrate its arrival with annual festivals.

In Pacific Grove, California, huge masses of butterflies settle on spectacular "butterfly trees." A grove of such butterfly trees may hold millions of monarchs. On cold days, when the butterflies are at rest, they look like clumps of fluttering brown-and-orange leaves. On warm days, clouds of butterflies take wing to feed but return to the trees at night. Toward the end of February, the monarchs mate and begin their journey north. Monarchs may live for four or five months after leaving their wintering places, journeying for hundreds of miles before laying their eggs and dying.

The locust is another migratory insect. Locusts are the air travelers most dreaded by humans. The sudden arrival of a swarm of locusts darkens the sky; a large swarm may easily contain fifty billion insects. In a single day, the munching mass of insects can eat three thousand tons of crops. Moving across the land, the swarm often brings ruin and starvation to communities in its path. In the Bible, a huge swarm is called a plague of locusts.

The most common locust—and the one that causes the most destruction—is the desert locust. When the population of North African desert locusts is low, they are green and flightless, and do not swarm. For many dry years, the number of locusts stays about the same.

But when the rains come to the desert, the females lay batches of hundreds of eggs, many more than usual. The eggs hatch in the damp soil in about two or three weeks, and the population of insects suddenly explodes. As they grow older and molt, the overcrowded locusts turn yellow or orange, with heavy, dark markings. Soon they undergo a final molt and emerge as adults with wings.

*T*aking to the air in large groups, the locusts swarm westward
with the prevailing winds. Locusts have powerful muscles that enable
them to fly at speeds of more than ten miles per hour for up
to twenty hours at a time. In the air, a locust swarm looks
like a towering, dark cumulus cloud, and often reaches a
height of more than a mile. One large swarm may cover
hundreds of square miles, an area larger than all of
New York City.

Some swarms travel thousands of miles,
laying eggs and beginning new swarms along
the way. If the locusts find food, the swarm
continues to move. When the food runs
out, the locusts die. Sometimes swarms
are blown out to the Indian Ocean,
where they drown.

Spiders are not insects and have no wings. Still, some kinds of small spiders, found in many different places around the world, have a remarkable way of journeying through the air: "ballooning." The spider moves to a high place on a branch or a rock, stands on "tiptoe," and faces into the wind. Then the spider thrusts its abdomen up into the air and produces a silken thread from its spinnerets. As the wind pulls the thread, the spider produces more and more silk. Finally, the silk thread is long enough to catch the wind and pull the spider aloft. The spider lets go of the ground and, dangling from the thread, is blown into the air.

Once in the air, the spider is carried by the winds. Tiny ballooning spiders are very light—a hundred may weigh less than a single paper tissue. Their small size and light weight usually assure a safe landing. When the thread breaks or strikes a tree limb or the top of a hill, the spider drops gently to the ground. Some tiny balloonists have been found at altitudes of up to three miles; some have alighted on distant islands or on ships hundreds of miles from shore.

Unlike the spiders that travel only with the wind, bats are free-flying mammals of the night. At dusk in the warmer months of the year, bats flap into the air in whirling dark clouds. Many bats weigh only about as much as a small coin and eat half their weight in insects every night. Huge flights of Mexican free-tailed bats can number in the millions when they emerge from their nursery caves in Texas and New Mexico for a night's feeding. The bats quickly eat up the insects in the local area and may travel forty miles each night searching for food. About nine hundred different kinds of bats are known—ranging in size from a few inches to some with five-foot wingspans. These giant bats are fruit-eaters.

When the weather turns colder, some roosts of free-tailed bats fly hundreds of miles southward to Mexico, where they can feed all winter long. Many kinds of bats do not migrate at all. Instead, huge groups of bats seek out a sheltered place such as a cave or a deserted mine, and like bears and other mammals, go into a deep sleep called hibernation. Their combined body heat keeps the cave temperature from falling dangerously low.

Seeds are air travelers, too. Some plants produce very small seeds that are lightweight and easily carried away by a breeze. Other plants make "parachute" fruits containing seeds that catch the wind and are carried aloft. Still other plants produce winged seeds that whirl through the air.

Cattails are common plants in many places in the world. What looks like a cat's tail is actually a spike containing thousands of fruits. Each fruit has its own seed with a tiny group of hairs called a pappus. When the fruits are ripe, they break away and the pappi spread out in the air. A gust of wind carries them off in a burst of tiny parachutes.

Dandelion pappi form little white balls that blow away with a light breeze. Each pappus has a fruit with barbs at the end. The barbs catch on the ground when they land.

Milkweed plants have fruits called pods. In the spring and early summer, the pods are green and soft. But when they ripen in the fall, the pods are brown and crack apart on one side. Inside the dry milkweed fruit are hundreds of brown seeds, each with a cluster of hundreds of long white silky hairs. As the wind blows, the parachutes open, and the seeds are shaken loose and are carried off into the air.

Cattails

*Cattail seeds
breaking away
and spreading out
into the air*

Dandelion

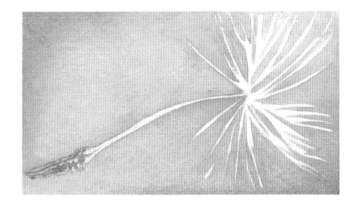

*Each dandelion pappus
is a tiny barbed fruit.*

Milkweed

*Milkweed pod
ripening and
opening*

One very puzzling migration behavior involves greylag geese. Every August, they gather in huge flocks to begin their seasonal migration to their winter home in India. But the geese are growing new feathers and cannot fly. So they begin their long journey by *walking*, traveling a hundred miles by foot across the Siberian plains. Along the route many of them are killed by human and animal hunters.

After two weeks, their feathers grown in, the geese take flight to the south. If they had waited only two weeks to begin their journey, the greylags could have flown the first hundred miles in a few hours. Yet each year, they migrate in the same strange way. No one knows why.

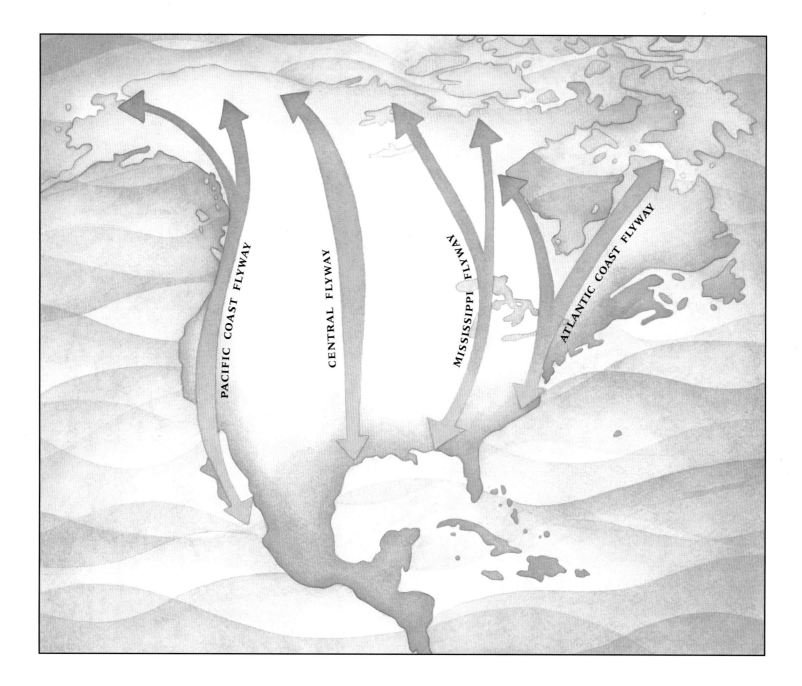

MORE ABOUT MIGRATION

*F*or many people across North America, the sights and sounds of flocks of wild geese and other waterfowl flying overhead in large formations mark the passage of the seasons from winter to spring and from autumn to winter. The total number of birds that migrate seasonally in North America is enormous. There are several hundred species, and more individual birds than the entire human population of the United States, Canada, and Mexico.

Almost every kind of bird follows its own schedule. There are four major flyways in North America: along the Atlantic Coast; the Mississippi River Valley; the eastern side of the Rocky Mountains (the Central Flyway); and the Pacific Coast. Some birds stop at certain places along the way to rest and feed, although these spots may change from year to year. Birds sometimes misjudge the weather and become snowbound in large groups. When the weather changes, the birds move on all at once.

One October, several sightings of blue geese showed how high and how fast the birds travel when they migrate. The first sighting was in the evening, when a very large flock of the blue geese was seen leaving from the southern tip of Hudson Bay. The following day, airline pilots reported seeing large flocks of the geese just north of Lake Huron, flying southward at heights of six thousand to eight thousand feet.

In fact, one of the planes was slightly damaged in a midair collision with a goose.

The next day, flocks of the birds were sighted over southern Illinois, flying south at an altitude of three thousand feet. On the following morning, blue geese began arriving on the Louisiana coast. In the sixty hours that had gone by from takeoff to touchdown, the blue geese had flown almost seventeen hundred miles at an average speed of nearly thirty miles per hour.

For a human observer, tracking migratory birds at night is difficult. Sometimes scientists watch the face of the full moon with binoculars. Perhaps once or twice an hour, the tiny, dark shape of a bird passes across the face of the moon, and the observer can tell the direction of movement. Using these observations, scientists try to estimate the approximate number of birds in the whole sky.

Radar that is used to locate airplanes can also be used to study bird migrations, even on a moonless or cloudy night. While radar can't tell one species from another, it can reveal the numbers and altitudes of birds moving across the sky out of human view. On a radar screen, birds can be tracked for many miles. Radar has shown that birds are able to fly a steady course in light side winds but not in strong ones. It has shown that birds fly straight when they go from night into day or day into night, but that they cannot continue on course in fog, thick clouds, or heavy rain.

We have learned many other things about bird migration from radar observations. Radar has shown that the air speed (the bird's speed, not counting the speed of following winds) of most small birds is about twenty miles per hour, although some larger birds travel at thirty to thirty-five miles per hour. Many birds, including snow geese and plovers, fly at altitudes between about three hundred and thirty-five hundred feet. But some other kinds of migratory geese fly far beyond the range of human vision from the ground, reaching heights of over ten thousand feet and sometimes even above twenty thousand feet.

Radar can help solve some mysteries about bird migration, but many puzzles still remain. For example, it's easy to see that migratory birds go to warmer climates in the fall and return in the spring. But just how do the birds know when to go? Some kinds of birds leave for the south in August or even July when temperatures are still high and food still plentiful. Just what is it that triggers the urge to migrate?

Early experiments seem to show that the changing length of the day triggers migration. But the equator has very little change in daylight from one season to the next. How do northern birds that winter along the equator know when to return north in the spring? After much more research, scientists have found that birds have a kind of yearly biological clock within them. The clock itself is corrected and triggered by outside events such as the changing length of day from one season to the next. The combination of a biological clock and some sorts of seasonal changes seem to be the cause of the bird migration.

Still another mystery is how birds find their way across huge distances. For two thousand years, people trained homing pigeons to become familiar with their surroundings so that they could return to their pigeon lofts from far away. Do some young migrating birds learn the migration route by flocking with adults on their first journey? How does a young seabird learn a route when it is flying over oceans that look the same from one spot to another? And how do birds that fly at night learn a route when they can't even see the ground?

Several different studies suggest the answer. In one experiment, starlings were kept in a special cage where the position of the sun could be changed by mirrors. During the spring migratory season, the birds flew to the north when the sunlight came from the correct position. But when the sunlight seemed to come from somewhere else, the birds changed direction to keep their bearings. Apparently, starlings use the sun as a compass to determine the direction to fly on their migrations. When it is cloudy and the sun is hidden, some migrating birds fly around randomly.

What about birds that migrate at night? In still another experiment, these kinds of birds were kept in a planetarium. When the position of the stars on the dome was changed, the night birds changed the direction of their movements. It seems clear that some birds can steer by the stars.

Another recent discovery is that some birds may use the earth's magnetic fields to help them find their way. Indigo buntings—birds that migrate at night and use the stars for guidance—were placed in cages surrounded by movable magnets. The birds shifted their flying patterns to follow the changing magnetic fields. Traces of iron were found in the brain tissue of some of these birds. Iron is attracted to Earth's magnetic poles. That may explain how it is possible for birds to be sensitive to magnetism. Still, none of these theories fully explains how and why birds migrate, and scientists continue to search for complete answers.

It's important to note that not all birds migrate. Small birds in particular can endure even cold winters so long as they remain active. Their increased activity means that they need more food. Not only is food scarcer in winter, but the shorter daylight hours mean there is less time to search for it. Although seed-eating birds, such as chickadees, can usually find enough seeds and berries even during the winter, insect-eating birds, such as swallows, cannot catch enough insects during the short day to last them through the long, chilly nights. So small insect-eaters are usually more migratory than seed-eaters. Seed-eaters that do migrate, such as the bobolink, often start their flights after sunset and fly through the night. They use the daylight hours to find food, and by flying at night they escape attack by birds of prey.

It is difficult to follow the movements of bats because they fly at night and are hard to see. But radar can track large groups of bats, and in some experiments, bats have been fitted with tiny radio transmitters to help scientists determine where they fly. Some bats have been shown to locate flying insects and other objects by producing a sound and then tracking the echo, although not all migrating bats can echolocate and they must use other senses. Scientists have shown that sight is an important aid to the bat in traveling long distances. Bats also become familiar with a local area and seem to rely on memory to find their roosts or feeding spots.

How do birds and other flying animals find their destinations across thousands of miles? How do they know when to take to the air? What makes them take such long and often dangerous trips?

For many animals, to live means to ride the wind. This can mean a one-way trip to a new place, a regular return trip according to seasonal changes, a full circle that completes an animal's life cycle, or an endless wandering. Although the powerful forces that underlie the windborne journeys of living things are still mysterious, scientists are slowly beginning to understand some of the puzzles.